Weekends With My Grandparents

By: Marlene Broussard

Copyright

Book Description

Here is a story of love and happiness as a little girl shares her loving experiences with her grandparents.

Weekends With My Grandparents is a story that accounts for how Amy, a little girl, appreciates her grandparents for loving her so much. She shares activities and events that she has with her grandparents. She feels lucky to have fun with both her mom's and her dad's parents.

This story will teach your little ones to appreciate the love and affection they receive. They will enjoy the adventures that Amy has with her grandparents. Also, family values, acceptance and bond are expressed in this book.

My name is Amy, and I am four years old.

I have two sets of grandparents. I visit them every weekend.

Last weekend I visited my dad's parents' house. Their names are Grandpa Will and Grandma Rose. They are one of my grandparents, and they are very loving.

I have fun with my grandparents. They show me pictures of my dad when he was so little, he had tiny legs and hands, just like I do.

Some pictures look like me, except I have pigtails. I laugh because his picture makes me very happy.

We watch movies, and Grandpa Will makes barbecue for dinner. Hmm, yummy! His barbecues are so delicious that I always ask for more.

However, no matter how full I am, I always save room in my tummy for my Grandma's yummy dessert. She makes them special.

I have exciting visits to my dad's parents' house. And when it's time to go, I wish I could stay more.

It's Saturday morning now, and I'm going to visit my Mama's parents for the weekend. My Mama's parents are Grandma Lena and Grandma Mary.

I am so excited! I'm happy that I will spend the whole weekend with them. I know they will be happy to see me too.

I never run out of fun things to do while visiting my two grandmas. My Grandma Lena enjoys baking, playing games, and reading books with me.

She also enjoys doing projects outside, like building tree houses for me to play in. She builds the best tree houses; they are always beautiful.

Grandma Mary enjoys outside projects too. In the morning, we pick corn and strawberries out of the garden. I love the scent of strawberries in the air.

We often eat sweet corn for dinner and strawberries with ice cream for dessert. And they are so delicious and yummy.

Both my Grandmas enjoy clothes shopping with me. I have fun picking out my favorite dresses, and sometimes we find matching shoes.

I always wear my new clothes to school on Mondays. My friends think I am very lucky to have such fun grandparents.

When it is Grandparents Day at my school, some of my classmates notice my grandparents are different from their grandparents.

They tell me I have two grandmas, and they notice Grandma Mary is not the same color as me and Grandma Lena.

I tell them I know. I tell them I am lucky to have two grandmas that love me so much, just as their grandparents love them.

My friends agree that we all are very lucky because they love their grandparents too. I also tell them I am lucky to have friends like them.

I love spending time with all my grandparents. They make me a very happy grandchild. And I know I have the best grandparents in the world.

Author Bio.

Marlene Broussard a native of Houston, Texas, has spent the majority of her life in the vibrant city of Seattle, Washington. As a mother of four and a grandmother to three delightful grandchildren, Marlene has been deeply involved in the joys and challenges of nurturing young minds. Her experiences in guiding and cherishing the unique stages of their lives have been a wellspring of inspiration for her writing. Embarking on a journey as a children's book author, Marlene brings a touch of personal authenticity to her stories. She prides herself on crafting her books personally, ensuring that each tale resonates with the warmth and sincerity of her own experiences. Rejecting the use of artificial intelligence in her creative process, Marlene collaborates with talented illustrators who share her passion and dedication to bringing stories to life through art.

Marlene's work is characterized by its ability to engage young readers with relatable activities and experiences. Her stories are not just about fun and adventure; they also gently delve into more challenging topics, offering parents a valuable tool for discussing sometimes uncomfortable but essential life lessons with their children. Through her books, Marlene Broussard seeks to ignite the imaginations of children, fostering a love for reading and learning that will last a lifetime.

www.ingramcontent.com/pod-product-compliance
Lightning Source LLC
Chambersburg PA
CBHW042113040426
42448CB00002B/248